Sekiya Miyoshi

David and Goliath

THE
PILGRIM
PRESS

Cleveland

Long ago in Israel lived a shepherd boy named David. Nothing pleased him more than leading his sheep to green pastures and lush mountain slopes. He loved his sheep.

But finding grass was getting difficult. Another nation was at war with his people. No one thought of others. Each side wanted to win and be the greatest. And what a terrible sight it was. All the green fields, forests, and houses were burned.

One day, David got so upset with the fighting that he shouted out loud,

"Why is life so difficult for us?"

And he heard a voice echo from the mountains, saying,

"People don't listen to God anymore. They are selfish. They think only of themselves and their wants."

"I won't forget to listen and think of others," David vowed.

But this tiny change didn't stop the fighting.
Even at night, war cries could be heard
somewhere. David's sheep were afraid and
wouldn't sleep. So he played his harp and
sang sweet, soothing songs to gently lull his
poor sheep to sleep.

Meanwhile, the king of Israel worried about his country's greatness—and he had terrible, throbbing headaches. He needed someone to soothe him.

Day after day, the king asked for help.

One day, an assistant said to him, "David, a poor shepherd boy, could help you. He plays the harp and sings so sweetly that all feel comforted."

So the king called David, his harp, and his sheep to the palace. Imagine the king's surprise. Whenever David played his harp and sang, the king's headache disappeared! So the king asked David to stay with him at the palace.

This bigger change didn't stop the struggle, either. Philistia, the neighboring country, challenged Israel to a showdown. But the Philistines had a giant man on their side.

David went to see the fight. As he watched,
a soldier came running up from the battle.
"I've never seen such a strong man,"
the soldier gasped. "He even claims to be
stronger and more powerful than God!"

This got David angry. How could any person be so selfish and claim to be better than God?

So David carefully hung his harp on a tree.
He took only his slingshot and a few stones
with him to fight this giant. One of his
favorite lambs followed him.

David walked toward the place where the
giant was. Suddenly a huge head rose
over the brow of the hill. Two eyes glared
at him angrily.

"What are you doing here, little boy?"
roared the giant. David was so terrified;
he wanted to run away.

The giant stood up, pointed a long spear at David, and snarled, "I am Goliath, the strongest man in the world. I'm even stronger than your God!"

"Oh, no, you're not!" David shot back, in a surprisingly steady voice. "No one is greater than God."

David gripped a stone in his
hand. Then he heard the same
voice that he had heard on the
mountain.
    "Throw the stone at Goliath.
Don't be afraid. For such big
boasters need to be brought back
to the ground."

David was amazed to hear himself
pray,
    "Please, God, help me do
what you want!"

David loaded the stone in his slingshot and swung it around his head. Whirr, whirr, whirr—and he flung it as hard as he could at Goliath.

Upward the stone shot like a rocket
and hit Goliath's forehead with a crack.

The huge man fell to the ground with a
thud. All the Philistine soldiers were
shocked and ran away in terror.

This big change stopped the fighting. Israel was peaceful once again. People weren't frightened any more. The land became green again.

David took his sheep back to the hillsides. He kept on playing his harp and singing to his sheep. He also kept on praying to God.

Much later when David was a man,
he was chosen to be king of Israel.
But he never forgot to pray each
day for his people.

He asked God to help them listen
to their hearts, never to boast or be
selfish, and to be kind to others at
all times.

David wanted his people to be
happy and live peacefully with one
another.

First published in North America 2001
by The Pilgrim Press
700 Prospect Aveue
Cleveland, Ohio 44115-1100 U.S.A.
pilgrimpress.com
Illustration and Original Text
Copyright © 1982 by Hisae Miyoshi
Original Japanese Edition "Dabide
to Oootoko" published in 1984 by
Shiko-Sha Co. Ltd., Tokyo, Japan
English text © 2001 The Pilgrim Press
Printed in China
06 05 04 03 02 01   1 2 3 4 5
ISBN 0-8298-1453-1